Down the Side of the Sofa

Written by Alison Hawes

Illustrated by Andy Hammond

I spy my lost car,
down the side of the sofa.

I spy my lost spoon,
down the side of the sofa.

I spy my lost sweet,
down the side of the sofa.

I spy my lost sock,
down the side of the sofa.

I spy my lost coin,
down the side of the sofa.

I spy my lost sandwich,
down the side of the sofa.